Catherine Brunner

4-

English
Works
Catherine Brunner
www.englishworks-cb.com

A Creative Borders Book

Write
from the
Edge

D1736568

Illustrated and Written

by

Ken Vinton

Edited by Pamela Espeland

free spirit
PUBLiSHiNG®

Works
for kids®

Copyright © 1996 by Ken Vinton

All rights reserved. Unless otherwise noted, no part of this book may be reproduced in any form, except for brief reviews, without written permission of the publisher.

Permission is granted for individual teachers to photocopy the illustrated border pages for individual classroom or group work only. Photocopying or other reproduction of these materials for an entire school system is strictly forbidden.

Library of Congress Cataloging-in-Publication Data

Vinton, Ken.
    Write from the edge : a creative borders book / illustrated and written by
Ken Vinton ; edited by Pamela Espeland.
        p.   cm.
    ISBN 0–915793–98–9 (alk. paper)
    1. English language—Composition and exercises—Study and teaching
(Elementary)—Handbooks, manuals, etc. 2. Education, Elementary—
Activity programs—Handbooks, manuals, etc. 3. Creative activities and seat
work—Handbooks, manuals, etc. I. Espeland, Pamela, 1951– . II. Title.
LB1576.V56   1996
372.6'23—dc20   95–25102
                                                                                                          CIP

Design and production by MacLean & Tuminelly

10 9 8 7 6 5 4 3 2

Printed in the United States of America

Free Spirit Publishing Inc.
400 First Avenue North, Suite 616
Minneapolis, MN 55401-1724
(612) 338-2068
help4kids@freespirit.com
www.freespirit.com

Dedication

I'd like to dedicate this book to the people in my life who not only inspire me but also allow me the space to create—my family: Ali, Ryan, and my wife, Mary Ann.

Contents

INTRODUCTION
1

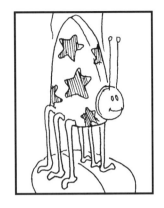

Paints, pens, markers, chalk, pencils, charcoal, computers . . . strange companions, or similar tools? They are similar because they can all be used for writing. You may want to have some of each on hand as you introduce your students to *Write from the Edge.*

Creativity shows its colors serendipitously. You never know when it's going to arise or what will awaken the wonderful beast. As teachers, part of our job involves encouraging creativity in our students. We try to provide them with time and materials, an environment and an audience conducive to creativity, because we know that creativity offers many rewards. Creative students, when given the chance to discover, explore, and develop their creativity, are happier, more interested, more motivated and involved. They enjoy expressing themselves, communicating with others, stretching their imaginations, and sharpening their skills.

Another part of our job involves teaching our students how to write. This is a skill they need to learn, and learning takes a lot of practice. *Write from the Edge* combines creativity with writing by giving students fun and interesting places to practice their ABC's, their P's and Q's, their sentences and paragraphs, outlines, essays, letters, stories, poems, reports, and journals. They may want to color in the borders; please let them. Of course, they can also use the pages for their own drawings and doodles. Starting from scratch can be frustrating and negative for the beginning artist. We can help novice artists by giving them a head start.

As artists draw from their environment, your students can extract information from a line, a saying, or a border. This knowledge can take the form of *satori* ("ah-hah," "I see"). It can also metamorphosize into a story that takes wing from the tiniest of chrysalises. My hope is that the appeal of the drawings, the hidden idea-fodder wrapped in the borders, will spur creativity and inspire students to weave a mystery, spin a fantasy, or try a rhyme or two. (Just as long as it starts them thinking and writing.) We all know that we get what we expect, so expect the best and you will be rewarded by excellence.

When I started this book, my main concern was to get students to think divergently, to step outside their own safe frameworks and try something new. As I drew more of the borders, the idea of letting students "direct" and produce their own mini-scripts emerged. I realized that the borders offered possibilities I hadn't even considered.

I've tried to include a wide variety of subjects to satisfy a diverse audience. I hope you have as much fun using these pages as I had coming up with them. Ideas and suggestions for using each border page ("Things to Do") are included on the facing page. Feel free to try your own ideas, and encourage your students to contribute ideas, too. A quotation related to the drawing is there to spur discussion and stimulate more ideas. "Discussion Questions" encourage students to look again at the drawing, think about how the subject relates to their own lives, use their imaginations, and sometimes indulge their silly sides.

You might use *Write from the Edge* for independent creative writing lessons or thematic lessons, by adding background and audio visuals or incorporating certain pages into the curriculum of the month. You might want to add lines to a page, especially if your students are learning their letters or need some structure for their writing. *Suggestion:* Instead of adding lines by hand, take a piece of the writing paper your students use and cut it to fit inside the border. Fasten it down with small pieces of removable tape and make your photocopies.

Speaking of writing: The border drawings for *Write from the Edge* came easily to me; I've been making drawings all my life. But putting words to paper was another matter. I felt just like my students when they come down with a bad case of the "I Can'ts." So I took the same advice I give to them: "Do the best you can, ask people you know for help, and let the thing stand."

Here I go. Thanks for coming along.

Ken Vinton
Indiana, Pennsylvania

Around the World

"People Are Different. Expect It. Respect It."
From the "People Are People" program at
Hoffman Estates High School, Hoffman Estates, Illinois

Things to Do

Celebrating Differences. Think about the importance of recognizing and celebrating differences. Use this page to write about your ideas, feelings, experiences, hopes, wishes, plans, dreams . . . .

Reading Log. Keep a personal/class reading log of multicultural books. Use it to promote diverse reading in the future.

Poetry or Acrostic. Use "people," "multicultural," "diversity," "global," "differences," "celebrate," and related words as poetry-starters or acrostic-starters. Write about ideas and images generated by the theme word(s).

Biographical Sketch. Research people from diverse ethnic backgrounds whose contributions have benefited humankind. Write a brief biographical sketch of one person, or use this page as a cover for a booklet of sketches.

Family Tree or History. Research your family history and draw your family tree. Or research your ethnic background and write biographical sketches of your parents, grandparents, great-grandparents, etc.

Where Did You Get Those Eyes? Why are blue eyes, brown eyes, green eyes, etc. the color they are? Research to find out. Where did your eye color come from? If you don't already know, ask your parents or other relatives.

Fingerprints. Fingerprints, like snowflakes, are unique. Why? Find out and write about what you learn.

Discussion Questions

- Has there ever been a time when you were surprised by something you learned about another ethnic or cultural group?

- Has there ever been a time when learning something new changed your opinion of a particular group? How did your opinion change?

- What are three things you have in common with everyone else in the world?

- Is it possible to have a "twin" somewhere in the world? *Tip:* Think beyond the usual meaning of the word "twin."

Basketball

"Sports is the toy department of human life."
Howard Cosell

Things to Do

In the Game. Use this page to write a brief essay on one of these themes: "If I was the world's tallest basketball player . . . ," "If I was the world's best shortest basketball player . . . ," "If I could play basketball for any team I wanted . . . ." Or come up with your own basketball-related topic.

History. Research the history of basketball (men's or women's) and write a brief report on your findings.

Word Lists. Primary school students: Write a list of words beginning with the letter B. Middle school students: Compile a list of sports-related words or a list of basketball jargon words.

Geography. Locate and study cities with professional basketball teams. You might follow a specific team and use this page to report results.

Math. List team statistics, do math computations based on the statistics, and illustrate math concepts related to the statistics.

Discussion Questions

- Why are basketball nets 10 feet off the ground?

- Do you think that the game of basketball should be changed in any way? *Examples:* Raise the basket to 11 feet? Widen the floor? Move the foul line back to 20 feet? Put more players on a team? Put fewer players on a team? How would your change improve the game.

- Which is better, a good small player (point) or a good tall player (forward)? Why?

- Why are basketball players called "cagers"? Why is the point area under the net called a "key"?

Laughter

"You grow up the day you have your first real laugh, at yourself."
Ethel Barrymore

Things to Do

The Importance of Humor. Explore humor and its importance in our lives. You might look in the library for good joke books or funny stories, then use this page to report on or list your findings.

Jokes and Funny Stories. Write your favorite jokes or funny stories. Compile them into a class booklet.

The Funniest Thing. Write about the funniest thing that ever happened to you. Give interesting (and funny) details.

Poetry. Write a "list poem." *Examples:* "Things that make me smile." "Things that make me laugh." "Things that make me roar with laughter." Create images—don't just list words on paper. *Example*: "My fuzzy little puppy covering my face with licks and kisses."

Biographical Sketch. Research the life of a great comedian or humorist, then write a brief biographical sketch.

Is Laughter Good Medicine? Is it true that people who laugh and smile live longer? Can you find any scientific studies that may support your hypothesis? Write about what you find.

Discussion Questions

- What would life be like if we woke up one morning and couldn't laugh anymore?

- What *always* makes you laugh, even when you're feeling sad?

- What is the silliest thing you ever heard or saw?

Poster Hangers

*"I think that I shall never see
A billboard lovely as a tree.
Indeed, unless the billboards fall,
I'll never see a tree at all."*

Ogden Nash

Things to Do

Billboard. Design a billboard advertising a new car, beverage, movie, vacation spot, service, TV program, etc. Or design a billboard advertising a new invention. Web ideas that show the things this new invention can do, what it looks like, etc., and write a paragraph about your invention from your idea web.

Class Billboards. Teacher: Cut the page into parts. (Depending on the size of your group, you might need to make several copies of the page.) Give a part to each student. Tell the student to write or draw something about himself or herself on the billboard part. Afterward, put the pieces together and post them as class billboards.

Teamwork. Think of an activity that takes a team of people to complete. Or think of a new activity or game that requires a team. Describe each person's role and how the team works together.

Christo. Research information on Christo, a Bulgarian-born artist who creates large-scale, temporary works of art by wrapping buildings, islands, etc. in fabric. List five important facts about his life or sketch a work of art similar to his.

Discussion Questions

- What are some advantages of teamwork vs. working alone? What are some disadvantages?

- Why are the people in this drawing covering the wall (if that's what they're doing)? What, if anything, might they be hiding?

- Are you for or against billboards? Give two reasons for your answer.

Construction Site

"Pardon my dust, I'm under construction."
Anonymous

Things to Do

Inventions. Use this page to spark all kinds of invention-related thinking and writing. *Examples*: Make a time line of important inventions. Create a new invention; describe it and its functions. Research how a new invention is patented. Research some inventions that didn't catch on.

Human vs. Machine. This page illustrates both mechanical and hand labor. Think about and talk about the need for both types. Historically, the introduction of a new labor-saving technology or machine has always created controversy. Research, discuss, and debate some of the issues related to this.

A Machine in Action. Think about (and perhaps sketch) a piece of machinery you have seen being used. Research its origins, purpose, function, etc. and write a brief report.

Pyramids. Research the types of construction and labor used to build the Pyramids. Write a brief report about what you learn.

Imagine This. Imagine a new use for an existing machine and write a description.

Discussion Questions

- How important is it to have a plan or a blueprint before beginning a project? How does having a plan relate to goal-setting?

- How important is communication in any type of project?

Alphabet Acrobats

*"Now I know my ABC's.
Won't you come and play with me?"*
Children's song

Things to Do

Alphabet Books. Make your own alphabet book. You might use your book to show what you know about a theme or concept you have studied. *Example*: "A is for Astronomy, B is for Big Bang, C is for Constellation . . . ." Or create an alphabet book about your state. *Example:* In Pennsylvania, you might use "A is for Allegheny Mountains, B is for Bituminous Coal" (important to Pennsylvania's economic development), and "C is for Charles, King of England" (who gave the land now known as Pennsylvania to William Penn). For each letter, write a sentence or two explaining your choice of subject. Or bring alphabet books to class (from home or the library) to share and display, then write about your favorite alphabet book(s).

Alphabet Lists. Make a list of nouns, verbs, adjectives, etc. for one or more letters of the alphabet.

Cryptograms. Create your own secret code. Write a coded message on the front of this page . . . and code-breaking tips or secrets on the back.

Gymnastics. Research gymnastics and their importance in the Olympic Games. Or research and report on your favorite gymnast(s).

Discussion Questions

- What kinds of information can be found in alphabet books?

- How does this page illustrate the concept of teamwork? Of cooperative learning?

- "A solid building starts with a good foundation." True or false? How can you relate this saying to other parts of your life—school, friends, family?

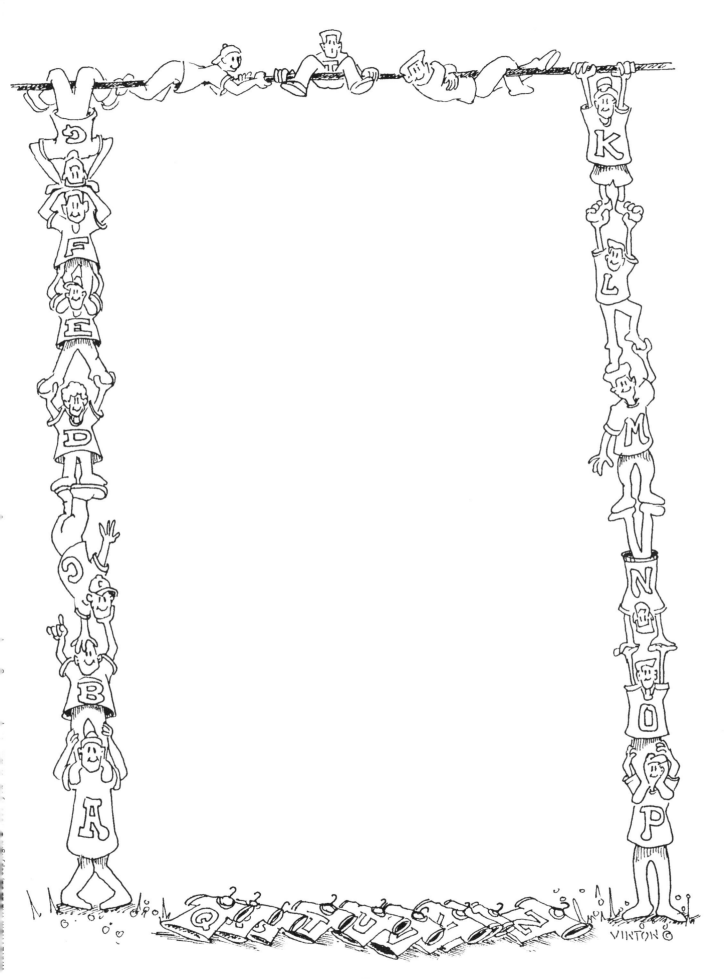

Circle of Friends

"For memory has painted this perfect day
With colors that never fade
And we find at the end of a perfect day
The soul of a friend we've made."

Carrie Bird

Things to Do

Games around the World. Research games that are played around the world. Share your findings by writing about the origins and rules of the games, then teach others how to play. Or research various types of ethnic dances and report on your findings.

Friends. Bring in books, poems, posters, etc. on friends and friendship. Use them as idea-starters for a story, essay, or poem.

What Makes a Good Friend? Make a list of 5–10 qualities you value in a friend. If you like, do this project with a friend. What ideas do you have in common? What qualities do you share?

Best Friends. Write a letter to your best friend. Tell him or her why your friendship is so important to you. (You don't have to send the letter if you don't want to . . . but maybe you'll want to.)

Togetherness. Write lists of things that are more fun to do as a group . . . or can't be done alone.

Discussion Questions

- Can you remember the last time you played Ring-around-the-Rosie? How old were you? Where were you? Who were the other people who played with you? Can you remember other games you played as a child?

- What are some other reasons why people might form a circle?

Crazy Day

"Imagination and fiction make up more than three quarters of our real life."
Simone Weil

Things to Do

What's Happening? Write about what you think is happening in the drawing. Expand your vision beyond the borders and also beyond the time pictured in the drawing. *Examples:* Is there anyone inside the window with the flower box? What will happen when the diver jumps off the platform?

Story Starters. Can "impossible" or unlikely events (such as a bird bowling in a tree) make good stories? Choose one element from this page and write a short story about it. Or write a story based on several (or all) elements from this page. You might start at either top corner, then create a story that shows "cause and effect" from one character to the next in sequential order.

Character Sketches. Give each character in the drawing a name and a personality. You might describe something about the character that can't be seen here.

The Perfect Job. Write about what you would consider to be the "perfect job." What would your responsibilities be? Your hours? Where would you work?

Career Shadowing. Choose a person in your community to "shadow" during a typical day at work. (Teacher: You'll need to arrange this ahead of time and get the appropriate permissions.) Afterward, write about the person you "shadowed" and describe his or her job responsibilities. Is this a job you might like to do someday?

Discussion Questions

- Albert Einstein once said, "Imagination is more important than knowledge." Do you agree or disagree? Explain.

- What gets your imagination going? What stimulates your thinking and makes you feel creative?

- Imagine that the round fruit in the drawing is "creativity fruit." What would happen if you planted some a) on the moon, b) in the Dead Sea, or c) at M.I.T. (Massachusetts Institute of Technology) or Harvard?

Big Hair

"Fashion is made to become unfashionable."
Coco Chanel

Things to Do

Styles and Fashions. Research different hair styles (or fashion styles) over the years. Write a brief report or a list of interesting facts.

Eek! Write about a "hair-raising" experience from your life.

Dreams. Make a collage inside the hair border showing the characters' dreams. Or write descriptions of the dreams.

Personal Experience. Write about a time when you needed someone else's "head" to help you solve a problem.

Discussion Questions

- Do you think that hair styles and fashion styles reflect the mood of the times? Give examples of current fashions and trends and explain how they relate to the present day.

- How important is hair in our culture? *Tips:* Think about commercials and advertisements for hair care products, baldness treatments, etc.

- Are two heads better than one? Is there ever a time when nine heads are better than one? How many heads are too many?

True Love

*"In our life there is a single color . . .
which provides the meaning of life and art.
It is the color of love."*

Marc Chagall

Things to Do

Love Story. Write a love story about the characters shown in the drawing. Or write any words that you feel go with the pictures.

Favorite Cartoonist. Pick your favorite cartoonist, study examples of his or her work, then try to duplicate his or her style. Bring in examples of the cartoonist's work to show along with your drawing. Middle school students: Collect political cartoons, then create your own political cartoon that is relevant to your life, times, issues, and/or environment.

Storyboard. Make a three-panel storyboard illustrating something from your daily life.

Flip Book. Create a cartoon "flip book" to show action.

Character Development. The series illustrations on this page depict the visual development of two characters. Choose a character from a book who makes a major change as the story progresses. Write about that character and describe the events that cause him or her to change.

Discussion Questions

- *Simplification* and *exaggeration* are two common techniques used in cartooning. Why do you think they work? What makes them effective? Why is your eye drawn to them?

- Some cartoons are very simple, yet they communicate a great deal through lines, shapes, and shadows. For example, how do cartoonists communicate that a character is male or female? Study the work of several cartoonists. What are some of the different ways they communicate the gender of a character?

City Scene

"It's a beautiful day in the neighborhood."
Mr. Rogers

Things to Do

City Mouse, Country Mouse. Research life in the city vs. the suburbs, the suburbs vs. rural communities. Think about the differences. Write down some of your thoughts. Does our environment determine our lifestyle? You might want to read the children's story, "The City Mouse and the Country Mouse," for ideas (or for fun).

Marbles. Research the game of marbles. Where did it start? Where is it played? Find out the rules of two or more marbles games and write them down. (You might want to illustrate the rules with drawings of different types of marbles.) Teach a friend how to play. Or invent your own game of marbles. Come up with a game goal, directions, and rules. Design your game pieces.

Pigeons. Find and list facts about pigeons. Do they live only in cities? If so, why? Or pretend you're a pigeon on a windowsill in this drawing. What stories can you tell about the people who live in the apartment buildings?

Discussion Questions

- Many "mom-and-pop" neighborhood stores are being replaced by chain stores and malls. What has been lost from this change? What has been gained? You may want to talk to a grandparent or other adult to get his or her opinion.

- What would it be like to grow up without grass? Or, if you live in the city, what *is* it like? What are some of the differences? *Example:* Suburban/country kids play baseball; city kids play basketball.

- Many cities have their own ethnic communities—"Little Italy," "Chinatown," etc. Why do you think ethnic groups tended to stay together when they settled in America? Can you think of any examples from the history of your own community?

Dinner Table

"It's a very odd thing—
As odd as can be—
That whatever Miss T. eats
Turns into Miss T."

Walter de la Mare

Things to Do

Setting the Table. Where do our "rules" for setting the table come from? Research this topic, then write about or list some of the rules. Or report on an interesting fact or finding. *Example:* Where did the fork and spoon originate? Which came first?

Dream Dinner Party. If you were about to sit down at the table in the drawing, what would you want to eat? Who would you want to sit next to or across from? Describe your idea of a "perfect dinner."

Where Is Everybody? The places are set, but there's no one at the table! Where is everybody? Write a story that answers this question. Your story might be funny . . . or it might be scary.

On the Menu. Imagine that this page is a restaurant menu. Give your restaurant a name, then write the menu for today. Be sure to include appetizers, main dishes, and desserts.

Dining Rooms. Are dining rooms a thing of the past? Where do most people today eat their meals? Survey your friends and neighbors. Record your findings on a chart or a graph. Write a brief report.

Discussion Questions

- Should homes today have separate dining rooms? Why or why not?

- How often does your family eat a meal together? Do you wish you could do this *more* often or *less* often?

- How is dinnertime different today than it was in your parents' generation? Your grandparents' generation? How has this affected family communication?

- Has your family ever solved a problem, made an important decision, or planned a family event during a meal together?

- Are good manners important? Why or why not?

- Is it true that you are what you eat? Does it matter what you eat? Explain your answer.

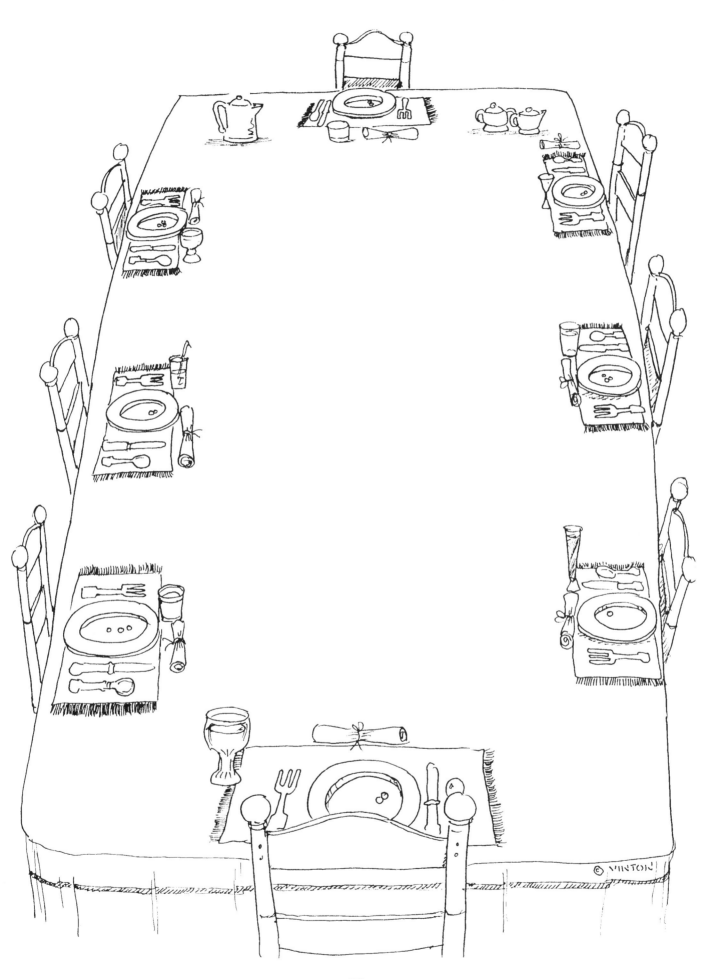

29

Corral

"Don't fence me in."
Popular song

Things to Do

Gone! Sometime late last night, all of the animals in this corral disappeared! Write about what kinds of animals they were and why they're no longer in the corral. Let your imagination go.

A New Breed. Create a new animal to live in the corral. Draw it and write about it. What does it look like? What does it eat? What sounds does it make?

Do We Need Fences? Fences, boundaries, borders—do we really need them? Are they useful, or are they confining? List examples to support your opinion.

Cowboys and Horses. Research and write about the history of mustangs and the cowboys who "broke" the wild horses. Or research your favorite type of horse. Draw it inside the corral and write a brief description or list interesting facts.

Discussion Questions

- In one of Robert Frost's poems is this line: "Good fences make good neighbors." Do you agree or disagree?

- Do we create fences in our minds?

- How did the fence change the American plains?

- What are corrals used for? Why do they have only one exit?

- Have we domesticated some animals so much that they can never be returned to the wild?

Condemned

"The optimist sees the doughnut
But the pessimist sees the hole."
McLandburgh Wilson

Things to Do

What Happened Here? Write about the events leading up to this scene . . . and tell what the dog and the cats (there are *two* cats) are doing here.

Earthquake! Research earthquakes. You might want to focus on one or more major earthquakes in history. Choose something from your research to write about—as a report, an essay, a letter from a witness or survivor, a news article, or whatever form you choose.

For Sale. You're a Realtor, and it's your job to sell this apartment building, no matter what shape it's in. Create an advertisement that makes it sound appealing.

If I Had a Hammer. Your family is considering moving into this building. Make a list of repairs that need to be done before you start packing.

You're the Architect. Come up with a list of challenging spelling words about architecture. Include definitions.

The Three Little Pigs. Rewrite the story of "The Three Little Pigs." This time, the brick house tumbles down and the straw house stays standing. Give reasons for these story twists.

Discussion Questions

- Would you rather live in an apartment building, a town house, or a single-family home? Discuss the pros and cons of each. Create a Venn diagram for comparison and contrast.

- Does a disaster such as an earthquake ever have a positive outcome? What about when cities are rebuilt?

- Is it better to rebuild something that has been badly damaged, or to start over from scratch? What about a building? A city? A relationship?

Other
your dream house
your real house

Rodeo

"Last night as I lay on the prairie
And looked at the stars in the sky
I wondered if ever a cowboy
Would drift to that sweet bye and bye."

"The Cowboy's Dream"

Things to Do

Rocking Horse Rodeo. Write a newspaper article announcing the Rocking Horse Rodeo shown in the drawing. The participants are all 11 years old or younger. What events are scheduled for them? Or give each character a name and write a story about their day.

Rodeo. What is a rodeo? Find out and write about your findings. List some events that would take place at a typical rodeo.

Classroom Rodeo. There are other kinds of rodeos besides bull-riding, calf-roping, bronco-busting rodeos. *Example:* Some communities have bike rodeos. You've just been put in charge of planning a classroom rodeo. Write a radio advertisement about it.

A Day in the Life. What happens during a day in the life of a cowboy or cowgirl? Find out. Write a story featuring a character you create.

Bales of Hay. Find out why and how hay is made into bales. What is the reason for baling hay? What special machines are used? Write about your findings.

Ten-Gallon Hat. Research the history of the ten-gallon hat. Does it have any special functions? Design a new kind of hat and describe it in words and drawings.

Discussion Questions

- What is a lasso and what is it used for?

- Did you ever play "cowboy" or "cowgirl" when you were younger? Why do you think little children enjoy that kind of play?

- What is your opinion of branding animals? Is it necessary? Is it cruel? Can you think of a better way to mark animals for identification?

Castle Towers

"It is a pleasure . . . to stand in the window of a castle."

Francis Bacon

Things to Do

Who Lives Here? What kinds of characters/creatures live in these castle towers? Why are the towers face-to-face? Use your imagination to write a story.

Castle. Read David Macaulay's book, *Castle.* Write down five interesting facts you learn from this book.

Create a Creature. Create a new mythical creature that lurks in the countryside surrounding these castle towers. Write about the mischief it causes.

Barbers. During the time when people lived in castles, barbers had many more responsibilities than they do today. Research this subject and write a report.

Discussion Questions

- Do you really think that damsels (young women) were hidden or imprisoned in castle towers?

- Why did castles have towers?

- Many castles had drawbridges and moats. Why?

- Are there fire-breathing dragons hiding in this border? Describe one.

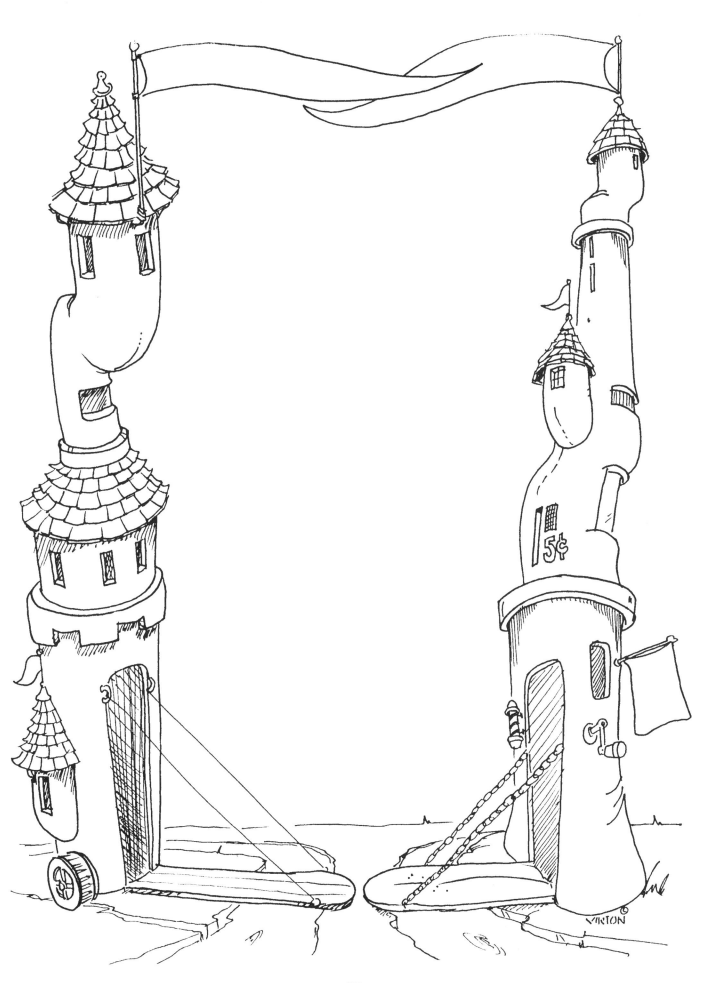

37

Forest

"The clearest way into the Universe is through a forest wilderness."

John Muir

Things to Do

The Three Little Stumps. If these stumps could talk, what would they say? Write a story with dialogue.

Homeless. What forest creatures might have lost their homes when the trees were chopped down? Use an encyclopedia or other reference book(s) to check your facts. Write about what happens when a forest loses its trees.

Habitat. Research forest habitats. Write about how the forest supports animals, plants, and insects.

Endangered Species. Spotted owls, snail darters, cranes . . . . Can you think of any other endangered species? What are their rights, compared to the rights of people who own the forest or earn their living from it? Take a viewpoint and defend it on paper.

Tree Products. What are some of the products made from trees? Think in terms of wood, sap, leaves, fruits . . . . Make a list. Add interesting facts. *Example:* How many toothpicks can be made from a single tree?

Arbor Day. What is Arbor Day? When is it? Find out and write a report. Plan to plant a tree on the next Arbor Day.

Discussion Questions

- Who really owns the forest?

- What is deforestation? How does deforestation affect the ozone and oxygen levels on the planet?

- If a tree falls in the forest and no one is around to hear it, does it make a sound? (This is an old philosophical question that has been much discussed for many years!)

Tall Houses

"A house is a machine for living in."
Le Corbusier

Things to Do

Who Lives Here? What kinds of people (or creatures) live in these houses? What do they look like? What are their names? What do they do for fun? Describe at least three people (or creatures).

Feelings. Imagine that the houses in the drawing have feelings. What are those feelings? What stories could the houses tell? Write a story as told by one of the houses.

Attic Treasures. You're exploring the attic of one of the houses. What treasures do you find? Write about your discoveries.

What Was It? There used to be something between these two houses. What was it? What happened to it? How long ago? Solve the "mystery" and write about your solution. Draw the "something" in the space.

Different Houses, Different Homes. Make a list of different types of houses. *Examples:* bird house, dog house, adobe house, igloo, earth-sheltered house, etc.

The Parts of a House. Learn about 5–10 different parts of a house. *Examples:* dormers, eaves, gables, peaks, foundation, studding, framing, corbels, cantilevers, etc. Write brief definitions of each. Make a list of at least 5–10 different parts on your house or houses near you.

Dream House. You have been given the opportunity to build your dream house. You can build any kind of house you like, with anything in it you want. Draw and/or describe your house.

Discussion Questions

- Does a house make a home? What's the difference between the two?

- What makes a good neighborhood—the houses/apartment buildings in it, or the people who live there?

- What kind of neighborhood do you see yourself living in as an adult? Will it have houses? Apartment buildings? Skyscrapers? Tents?

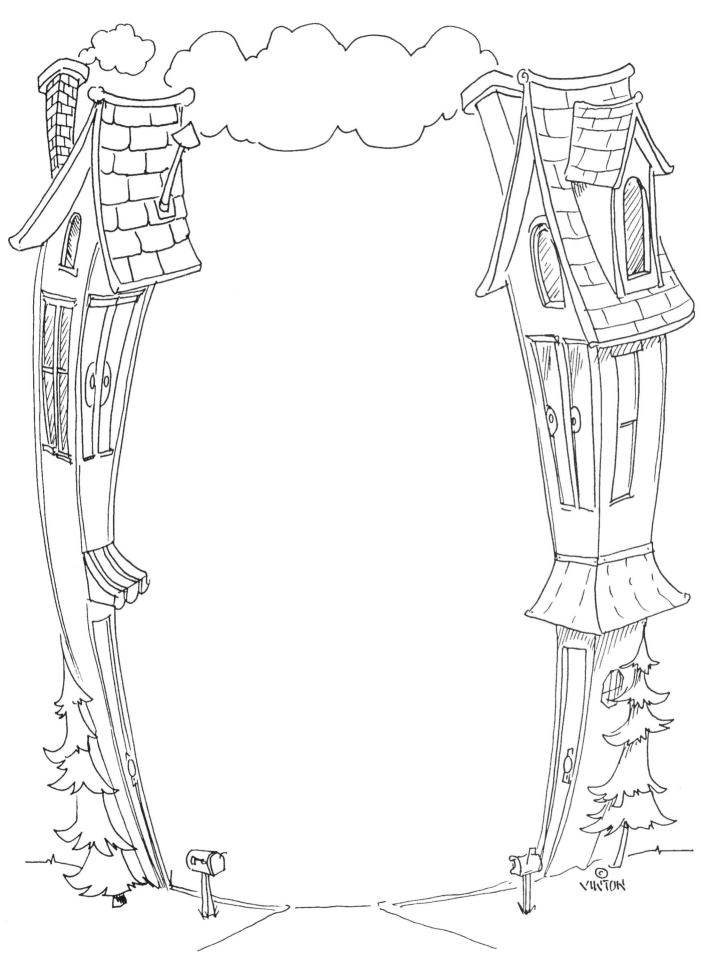

Stairways

*"As I was going up the stair
I met a man who wasn't there.
He wasn't there again today.
I wish, I wish he'd stay away."*

Hughes Mearns

Things to Do

Telling the Story. Where are these steps going? Why is there a hole in the floor? Who (or what) lives in the hole? Answer these questions in story form.

Setting the Stage. Imagine that this page shows a stage set. Write the stage directions for the first scene of a play. Describe the lighting, music, and sounds. Who is waiting off stage to enter the scene?

Goal Setting. Decide on a personal goal you want to reach. Describe in writing the steps you will take to achieve your goal.

Flights of Fancy. Research different types of stairways (spiral, suspended, etc.). What is the standard riser height? List this fact and three more you learn from your research.

Going Up, Going Down. Find out about other ways of going from level to level. Who invented the escalator? Who invented the elevator? When and where was the first elevator installed? Why do fire stations have poles instead of stairs? Write about your findings.

M.C. Escher. Go to the library and find a book on the graphic work of Dutch artist M.C. Escher. Find at least three works that remind you of this drawing. List their titles and describe what they have in common with the drawing. *Hint:* Look for *Ascending and Descending* and *Möbius Strip II—Red Ants* for starters.

Discussion Questions

- Can we get anywhere without taking a first step?

- How many steps do you have in your house? Estimate and check.

- What is a Möbius strip? How is it related to the stairs in the drawing?

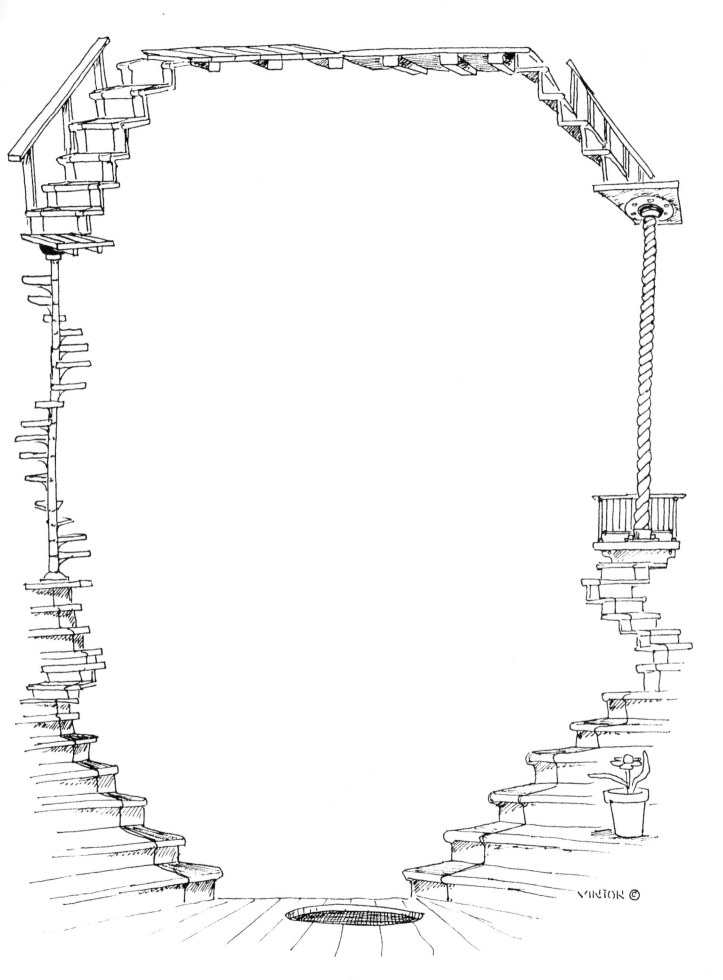

43

Incredible Engine

"There she is—the great engine—she never sleeps."
William Makepeace Thackeray

Things to Do

What Is It? Study this machine. What is it? What does it do? What is it called? Imagine that you're the inventor, and you're trying to convince investors to give you the money to mass-produce your invention. What will you tell them? Write a short speech.

Going Beyond the Drawing. Develop a machine even wilder and more fantastic than the one in the drawing. Describe its functions in writing.

Is It Human? When people attribute human qualities to an animal or an object, this is called *anthropomorphism.* Use some anthropomorphism on this machine. Give it a name, a personality, a voice. Give it likes, dislikes, and feelings. Write a short story about it.

Discussion Questions

- Why do you think people so often refer to machines as if they were female? *Examples:* "My car is acting up; I have to take her into the shop . . . ." "Give her some gas . . . ." "She's a great little power boat."

- Do you think that all possible machines have been invented, or are there more yet to come? Give some reasons for your answer.

- Could pollution from the machines of today's world destroy the environment (from the polar ice caps to the tiny plankton in the sea), or are environmentalists just "blowing smoke"?

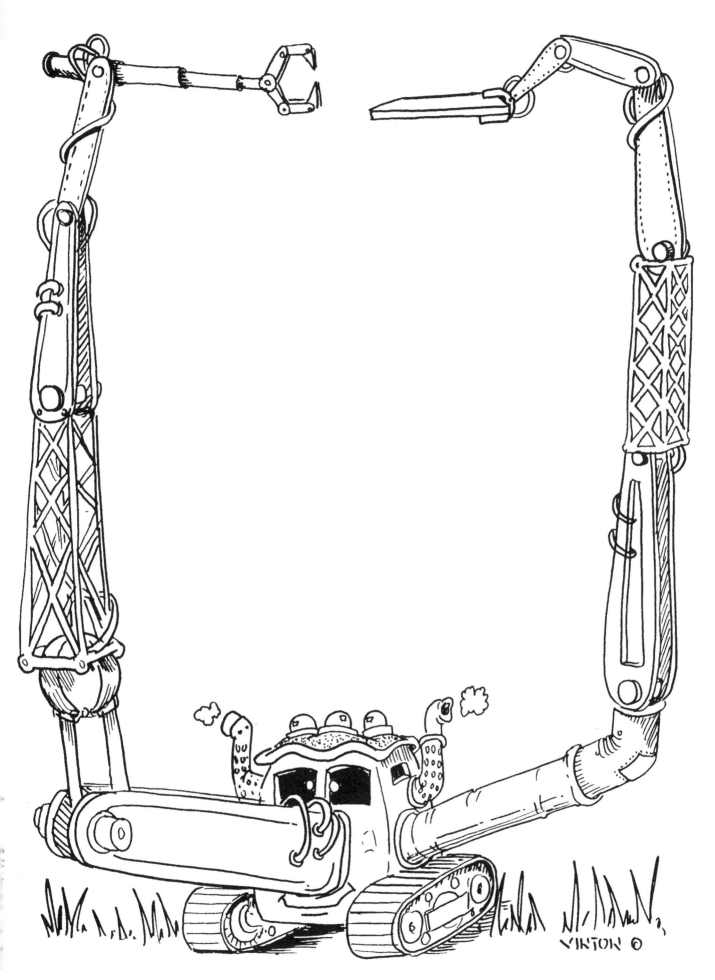

VINTON ©

Used Cars

*"Take most people, they're crazy about cars . . .
and if they get a brand-new car
already they start thinking about
trading it in for one that's even newer."*

J.D. Salinger

Things to Do

Are They Related? What do you notice about these cars and vans? Do they look alike? If so, are they related? What are they doing? Write about this scene.

For Sale. Create an advertisement to promote this line of vehicles. What are their special features? What about them will make people want to buy them?

The Car of Tomorrow. Design the automobile of the future. Describe it in words. Draw it.

The People's Car. Research the history of the Volkswagen. List five interesting things you learn about this popular car.

Discussion Questions

- Are all things that look the same really the same? *Examples:* Volkswagens, twins. What differences can be hidden?

- When is it good to be the same as someone else?

- Can you think of something—anything—that is truly unique and one of a kind?

- Is individuality always a positive quality?

49

Up, Up and Away

"Flying may not be all plain sailing, but the fun of it is worth the price."
Amelia Earhart

Things to Do

Up You Go. Brainstorm a way to lift yourself into the air. Describe how you will do this. What materials will you need? How high will you go? How will you get back down?

Time Line. Research the history of transportation. Make a simple time line.

Evolution. Choose one type of transportation (wagon train, airplane, ship, etc.). Research its evolution and write a report.

Story Time. What stories do this drawing tell? What about "The Little Airplane That Saved the Day"? "The Last Balloon Ride"? Study the drawing until you "see" a story, then write it down.

How Many? How many modes of transportation can you find in this drawing? List them, then list ways in which they are different from each other.

Discussion Questions

- Humans have progressed from wheel travel to air travel. What's next?

- What are some of the changes that have taken place due to the invention of transportation vehicles?

- What's an "airhead"? Where do you think this word came from?

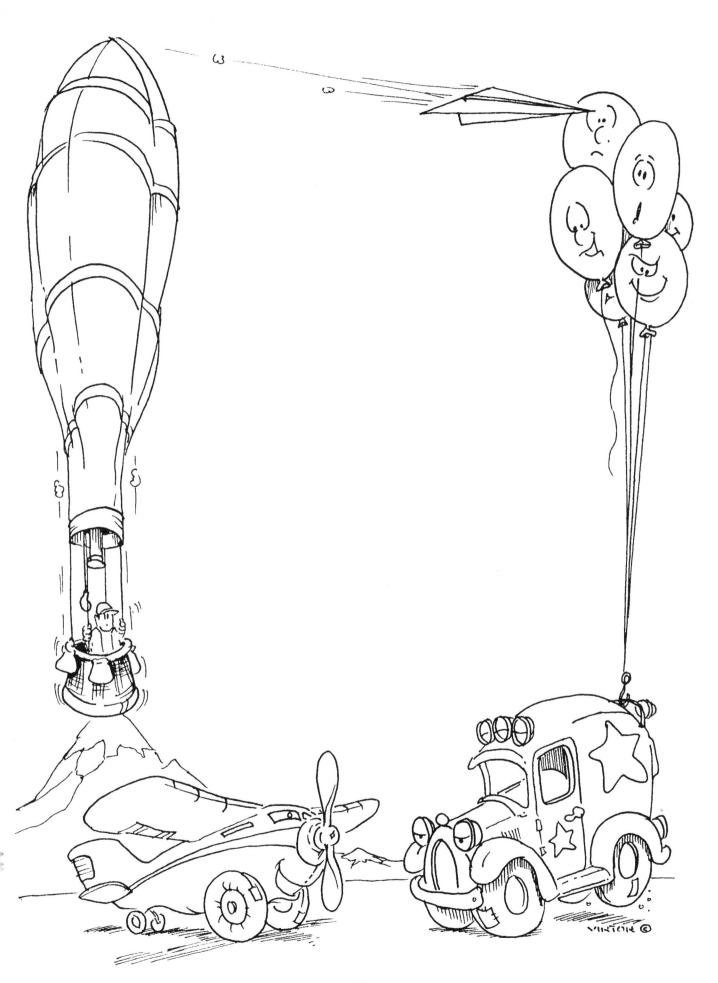

Circle Race

"If you don't know where you are going, you'll end up someplace else."

Leo Durocher

Things to Do

The Great Race. "The Great Race" would be a good title for a story about this drawing. So would "The Day My Car Drove Itself" or "The Fuel of the Century" or "The Amazing Acrobatic Automobile." Pick one of these titles, then write the story.

From Start to Finish Line. Research and report on a famous annual race. This might be a horse race, an automobile race, a bicycle race, or . . . .

Plan to Win. To get ahead, we need a plan. Without a plan, we go around in circles! Write a plan for accomplishing a personal goal in five "laps." Each "lap" should move you toward the "finish line"—your goal. Write your five-lap plan.

Discussion Questions

- Do you have a vision for your life? Is a vision the same as a plan?

- Do you ever feel as if you're going around in circles?

- What good does professional racing do? For example, who benefits from the Indy 500?

- Where would we be today without the automobile?

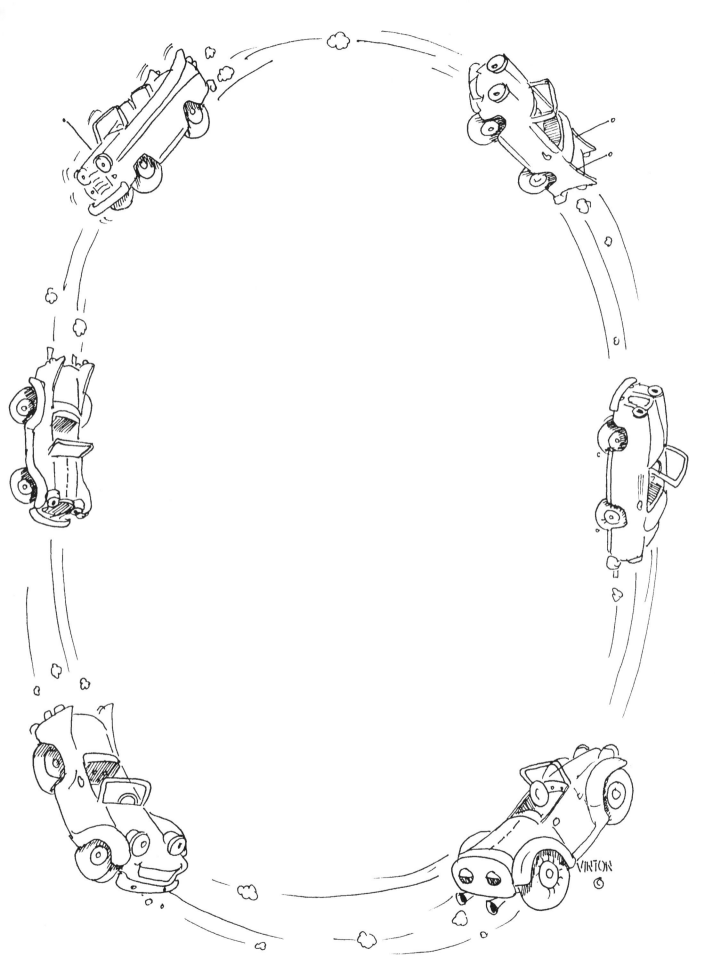

Tractor Truck

"Keep on truckin'."

R. Crumb

Things to Do

Mystery Truck. What strange load is this truck carrying? Where is it going and why? Could it be carrying a Top Secret load for the government? Write about this truck and its baffling contents.

Trucks. Research different types of trucks and how they are used. List at least five interesting findings.

Camper. This is a drawing of your new camping vehicle! Where will you go on your first camping trip? What will you bring?

The Explorers. Research the history of a famous explorer or team. *Examples:* Richard Byrd, Admiral Perry, Lewis and Clark. How did the explorers of old pack for a mission? What did they take? What were they looking for? What were some of their biggest problems? Write responses to one or more of these questions.

You're the Explorer. Pretend that you're an explorer going into unexplored territory. What have you packed inside your exploration vehicle? Write down your packing list.

Discussion Questions

- What does it mean when a truck is "overloaded"? Can people get overloaded?

- You've kicked yourself into four-wheel drive and now you're off the "beaten path." Where will you go? What will you do?

Airport

"The aeroplane has unveiled for us the true face of the earth."

Antoine de Saint-Exupéry

Things to Do

Airplane Adventures. This airplane has the look of accomplishment. It has gone places, done things, and seen things. Write about its adventures.

Time Travel. This airplane can travel through time. Where has it been? Who and what has it seen? Where (when) will it go next? Write a journal of its travels through time.

High in the Sky. Write a haiku or cinquain about the experience of flying. If you haven't ever flown in an airplane, write about how you imagine it would be.

Flying Words. Make a list of words associated with air travel. Add brief definitions. Find at least five words.

Flying Machines. Find and list interesting facts about dirigibles (zeppelins), helicopters, propeller planes, balloons, jet planes, rockets, and/or other flying machines.

What Next? After the jet, what next? Imagine and describe a new mode of transportation that can transport millions of people quickly, efficiently, and economically.

Breaking the Sound Barrier. Imagine that you are the Concorde, a jet that is able to travel at over 2,000 miles per hour. Describe how it feels to take off, break the sound barrier, and land.

Discussion Questions

- Why do airports have wind socks?

- Why does a pilot need to know the direction of the wind?

- Why is an airport called an airport? Can you think of a better word for it?

- Would you like to be a pilot someday?

- Can an airplane taxi? Where? When?

Caboose

*"The engine got most of the attention,
but the 'little red caboose' . . . was where the action was.*"

Donald Dale Jackson

Things to Do

Home on the Rails. Do the people in the caboose live on the train? Tell their story. Make it the "adventure of a lifetime."

John Henry. Read about John Henry, the American folk hero—"a steel-drivin' man." (Look for the song, "John Henry," in a book of American folk songs.) Write a report on what you learn.

Circus Train. This caboose is the last car on the circus train. Write about the people and animals riding on the train. Where is the train going next?

Campaign Train. You are running for President, and you're doing a "whistle stop" tour of America on board your private train. Write a campaign ad to write in the space, stating your qualifications for the job.

Discussion Questions

- What is the purpose of the caboose? Do trains still have cabooses?

- Where are they going in the drawing, and are they on the right track? Is there a "switching station" you can go to if you have been on the "wrong track" for a while?

- Is it always a bad thing to come in last? Are there some competitions where being last is best?

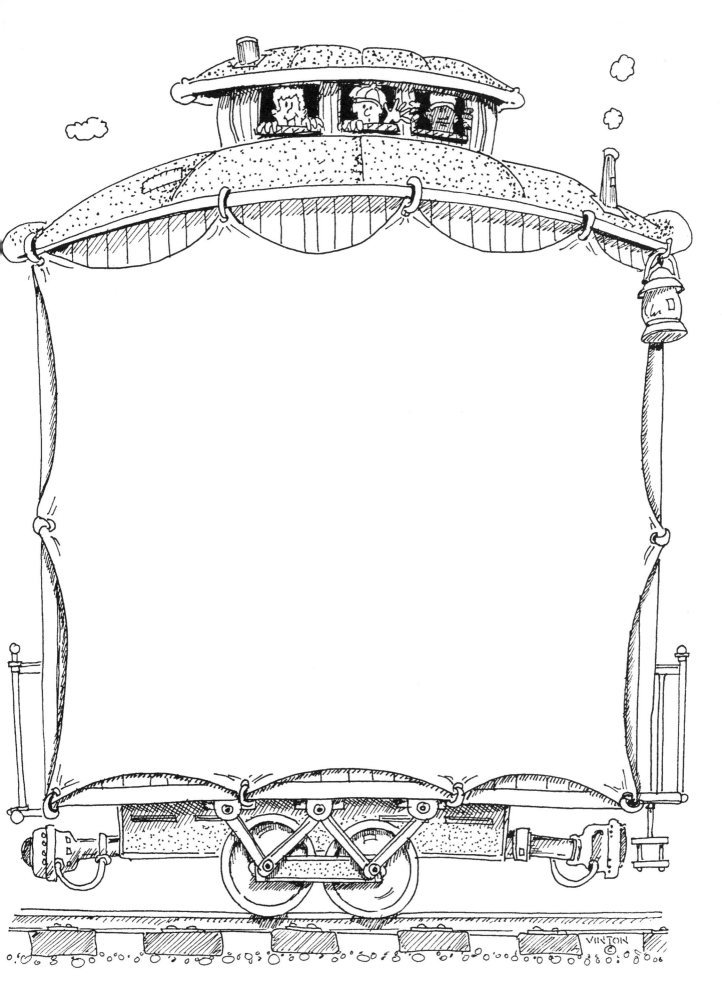

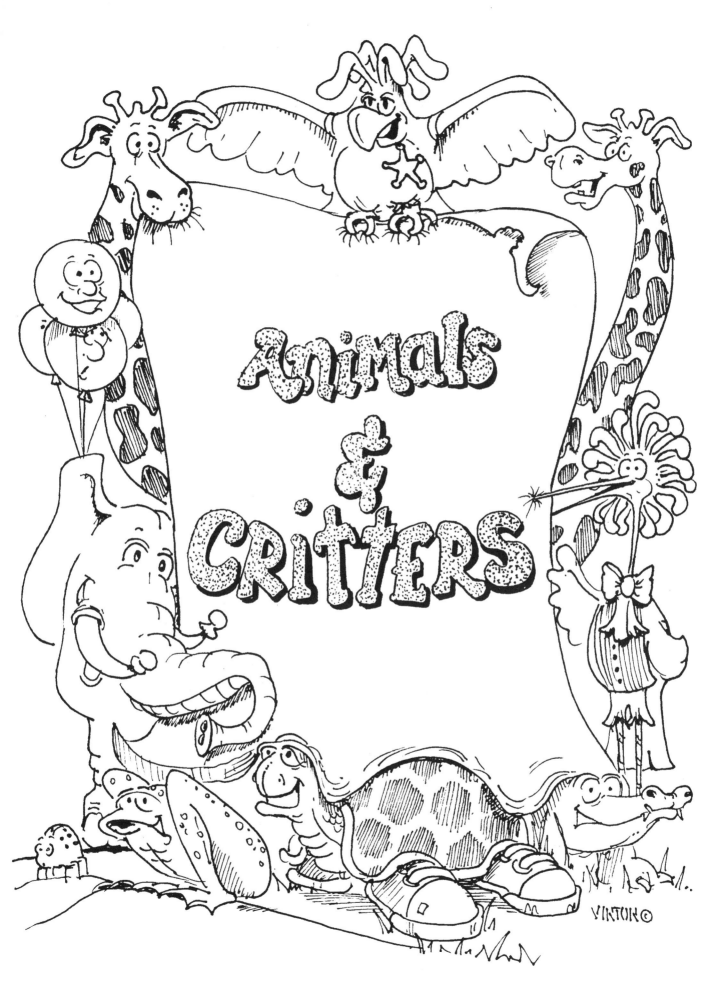

Teddy

"Nothing great was ever achieved without enthusiasm."
Ralph Waldo Emerson

Things to Do

Bear Story. Jeremy, the juggling bear of baseball, saves the day! Write about it.

Animal Training. Research how animals are trained and write a brief report on your findings.

Animal Acts. What kinds of animal acts are usually included in circus performances? Write about one—or invent a new one of your own.

Bear Facts. Research the different types of bears that are native to the United States. List at least five interesting facts you find. Or learn and write about the history of the Teddy Bear.

Bear Poems. Write a poem about your favorite bear(s).

Bear Day. You might want to celebrate bears with a special Bear Day. Use this page to write an invitation. Share bear poems, stories, and songs. Bring your favorite stuffed bear to class. Or you might bring in something else related to "bears"—maybe a Chicago Bears hat or T-shirt? (Do you know of any other bear mascots?)

Juggling. Find and list five interesting or funny facts about juggling. *Example:* Do jugglers juggle from right to left or from left to right? If you know how to juggle, write about how you learned.

Discussion Questions

- Is juggling a math skill? Explain.

- Do you think that animals should be trained to perform for people? Why or why not?

- Why are bears used in fairs, festivals, circus acts, and animal acts?

- Why do we dress animals in people's clothing? Do you ever dress your dog or cat in people's clothing?

- Is it important to be enthusiastic about everything you do?

VINTON ©

63

Snakes

"The only thing we have to fear is fear itself."
Franklin Delano Roosevelt

Things to Do

Facing Your Fears. Many people are afraid of snakes. If you are afraid of snakes, write about your fear. Where does it come from? What are two things you could do to become less fearful of snakes—or stop fearing them? If you're not afraid of snakes, think of something else you fear (spiders? heights? the dark?) and write about that instead.

Snake Facts. Find out at least five true facts about snakes and list them on this page. Put a star by the fact that surprised you the most.

St. Patrick. Find and read the story about how St. Patrick drove the snakes out of Ireland. Use this page to summarize the story.

Snake Poems. Find, read, and share a poem about snakes. Or write your own poem. Try to include some snake facts in your poem.

Snake Stumpers. Find out some myths and facts about snakes. Use them to write at least five true-or-false questions about snakes. *Examples:* "Snakes are slimy. True or false?" "Snakes can climb trees. True or false?" Have a "Snake Stumpers" contest in class.

Animal Personalities. We associate certain characteristics or personality traits with certain animals. *Examples:* Cats are curious; dogs are faithful. Name three animals. For each, list at least three characteristics or personality traits.

Discussion Questions

- Why are people so afraid of snakes?

- Why are these snakes so happy?

- Can snakes climb trees? How do you know?

- Would a snake make a good elevator operator?

- Would you like to be able to shed your skin? What would life be like if people could shed their skins?

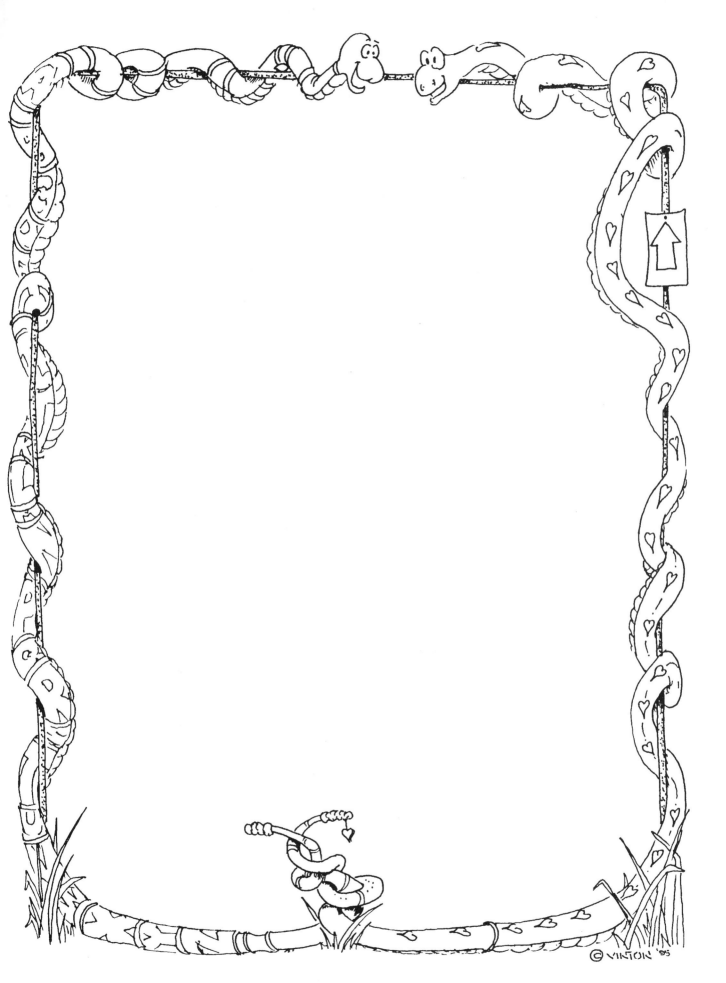

Dog

"The dog was created especially for children."
Henry Ward Beecher

Things to Do

Dog Tale. Write a story about your dog, if you have a dog. If you don't have a dog, write about the kind of dog you would like to have. Or write about why you *wouldn't* want to have a dog.

Doggerel. "Doggerel" is a word that means "bad poetry." Write a piece of doggerel about dogs.

Dog Tags. Make a list of words and phrases that include "dog." *Examples:* Dog Days, dog-tired, sick as a dog. Try to come up with at least five examples. Include definitions.

Owner Wanted. This puppy is advertising for an owner. Write an advertisement from the puppy's point of view. List the qualities it would like to have in an owner.

First Prize Pup. This puppy just won First Prize in a dog show. Why did it win the prize? Write about the puppy's special qualities and talents.

Flying Pup. This puppy has such big ears that it can fly! Write a story about the puppy's adventures.

Dog Facts. Find and list 5–10 interesting facts about dogs. If you like, you can research a particular breed of dog.

Discussion Questions

- What is "puppy love"? Why do we call it this?

- Do people train their pets . . . or do pets train their people?

- Since dogs communicate by barking, do trees communicate with their bark?

- A man named Andy Rooney once said, "The average dog is a nicer person than the average person." Do you agree or disagree? Explain your answer.

Early Birds

"The early bird gets the worm."
Anonymous

Things to Do

Home Alone. The Robin Twins are home alone. What kind of trouble can they get into? Use this page to write a short story about their adventures.

New Species. Scientists have just discovered a new species of speckled-egg, twisty-neck, bow-tied birds. Write an article describing the unusual habits of this new species. Give it a scientific-sounding name.

Bird Facts. Research a bird that is native to your geographic area. List 5–10 interesting facts you find about the bird, its habitat, and its habits.

Bird Journal. Choose a specific window in your home to use for bird-watching. Keep a list of the different types of birds you see over a period of a month. If you don't know the name of a particular type of bird, draw it or describe it in words. Ask your teacher or another adult for help figuring out what kind of bird it is.

Discussion Questions

- Is it true that the early bird catches the worm?

- Are you an early bird or a night owl?

- Which came first, the chicken or the egg?

- How do worms tie their shoes?

- Something unusual is happening in this drawing. What is it? *Hint:* Are the early birds trying to catch the worm . . . or is it the other way around?

Pig

*"This little piggy went to market.
This little piggy stayed home."*

Children's nursery rhyme

Things to Do

The World's Smartest Pig. This is a portrait of Quigly Einstein Sodbuster, The World's Smartest Pig. He just won the Piglitzer Prize for his new invention. What is it, and how will it help pigkind?

Super Pig. Here he comes to save the day! Use this page to write about his adventures.

Pig Facts. Research pigs. How many kinds are there? How long have pigs been domesticated? List at least five important facts about pigs.

Pigs in Literature. Can you think of examples of pigs in literature? Make a list and give brief descriptions. (Try to remember stories you read or heard when you were young.)

Are Pigs . . . Pigs? Pigs have a bad reputation for being dirty and greedy. Do they deserve this reputation? Why or why not? What are pigs really like? Find out and write a brief report.

Ham It Up! This pig is trying out for a part in a play by William Shakespeare. The play is called *Hamlet,* and the pig wants a *big* role. Use this page to write a scene for the pig to give during the audition.

Discussion Questions

- What other animals have bad reputations they don't deserve? If possible, give some examples of myths and facts.

- What happens when we get a reputation we don't deserve?

- What is a truffle? Is a truffle a trifle? What do pigs have to do with truffles?

- What is a pigsty? Has anyone ever called your room a pigsty? Why (or why not)?

Bugs

"Snug as a bug in a rug."
Benjamin Franklin

Things to Do

Bug ABC. Create a "Bug ABC" book. Try to find a bug for each letter of the alphabet. Draw it and list two or three interesting facts about it.

Bug or Insect? Is a bug an insect? Is an insect a bug? Find out and write about what you learn.

What Is It? One of the critters in this drawing is not a bug. Find it, find out what it is, and write a brief report on this kind of critter.

Giant Bugs. The bugs in this drawing are magical bugs that will one day grow to be giants. Write about their adventures.

The Bugs around You. Stake out a small section of grassy area by your school or home. Investigate to find out what kinds of bugs are in your "lot." Name them, draw them, describe them.

Invent-a-Bug. Invent a bug of your own. How many legs will it have? Will it have spots, stripes, or . . . ? How will it behave? Where will it live? Be creative, and don't be limited by "reality." This can be a fantasy bug with special features and abilities.

Future Entomologist? Look up the word "entomologist" in a dictionary and write the definition. Would you like to make entomology your future career?

Discussion Questions

- Why do some bugs have antennas? Is it because they don't have cable?

- Do bugs have communities? Towns? Mayors? Baseball teams?

- Is there someone in your life who bugs you? Describe this person and explain why he or she drives you buggy.

Rabbit

"Once upon a time there were four little Rabbits, and their names were—Flopsy, Mopsy, Cottontail, and Peter."
Beatrix Potter

Things to Do

Where's the Rest of It? This bunny lost its body! Draw it.

Rabbit or Hare? What is the difference between a rabbit and a hare? Find out and write about what you learn.

The Tortoise and the Hare. In the famous fable, the tortoise ("slow and steady") beats the hare in a race. Write a sequel in which the hare wins.

How the Rabbit Got Its Ears. Write a story explaining how the rabbit got its ears. For inspiration, read one or two of Rudyard Kipling's *Just So Stories.*

The Rabbit in the Hat. As part of their act, magicians often pull a rabbit out of a hat. Can you find out how this trick is done? Write about it or draw a description. Or research a famous magician (Harry Houdini? David Copperfield?) and write a brief article about his or her life. Or invent your own magic trick and give directions for doing it.

Albino Bunny. What is an albino? What causes albinism? Why is it so common in rabbits? Find out and write a brief report.

A Harebrained Scheme. What is a harebrained scheme? Have you ever come up with one? Write about it and tell what happened.

Discussion Questions

- Can you name a famous rabbit? (Think of books, television, movies, cartoons, etc.). Which famous rabbit is your favorite? Why?

- Have you ever had a "lucky rabbit's foot"? Why do people think that rabbits' feet are lucky? Are they lucky for the rabbits?

- What is the bunny hop? Have you ever been part of this dance? Was it fun?

- What's up, Doc?

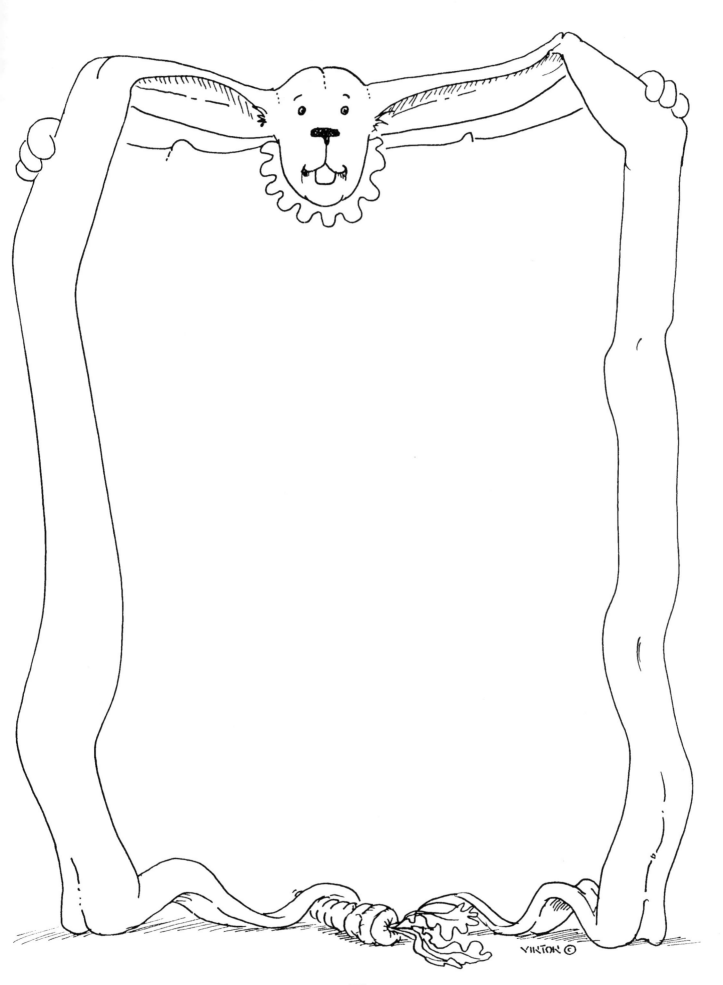

High Wire Critters

"Climb high
Climb far
Your goal the sky
Your aim the star."

Inscription on steps at Williams College,
Williamstown, Massachusetts

Things to Do

High-Wire Hero. Imagine that you're walking the high wire. Write about your feelings and the events leading up to this moment. Create a billboard at the bottom to advertise your stunt.

Critter Circus. The Critter Circus has come to town! Use this page to write a program describing the various acts the audience will see. You might also mention other acts that aren't visible on this page.

What's the Connection? All of these critters are related, and they all have a story to tell. Pick one or two and tell their stories. The stories should have something to do with where they are in the drawing.

Personal Achievement. Write about something you once did that you thought you'd never be able to do. How did you overcome your "mental blocks"? How did you feel afterward?

The Ladder of Success. When you think about "climbing the ladder of success," what does this mean to you personally? Answer this question, then list five steps on your personal ladder of success.

Discussion Questions

- Can you find different emotions in the faces of the critters pictured on this page? What emotions do you see?

- What about their body language? Do you ever use body language to communicate different feelings? Give examples.

- Are these critters professional performers or amateurs? What's the difference? How can you tell?

- Would this be a fun way to take a bath?

Traveling Turtle

"Whatever creativity is, it is in part a solution to a problem."

Brian Aldiss

Things to Do

The Turtle's Problem. This turtle had a problem. What was it, and how did the turtle solve it? Write about it.

The Turtle's Mission. This turtle has recently been hired by the government for a secret mission. Write about it.

You're the Inventor. The turtle on this page is your invention. Tell why you invented it and describe its special features and abilities.

All about Turtles. Research various types of turtles, their habits, their habitats, and anything else that interests you. Use this page to report on your findings.

Turtle or Tortoise? Is a turtle a tortoise? Is a tortoise a turtle? Find out and write about what you learn.

Discussion Questions

- You have just been given the opportunity to be fitted with special bio-robotic attachments. They won't hurt at all, and they will give you super-powers. Will you say yes or no? Explain your answer.

- If you say yes, what will you do with your new super-powers?

- Imagine that you can carry your house with you wherever you go. However, space is very limited! You can only bring three of your favorite things. What will you bring?

- What is made out of tortoise shell and is it legal?

- Why is the turtle in the picture wearing a helmet and pads? Are they knee pads or elbow pads?

78

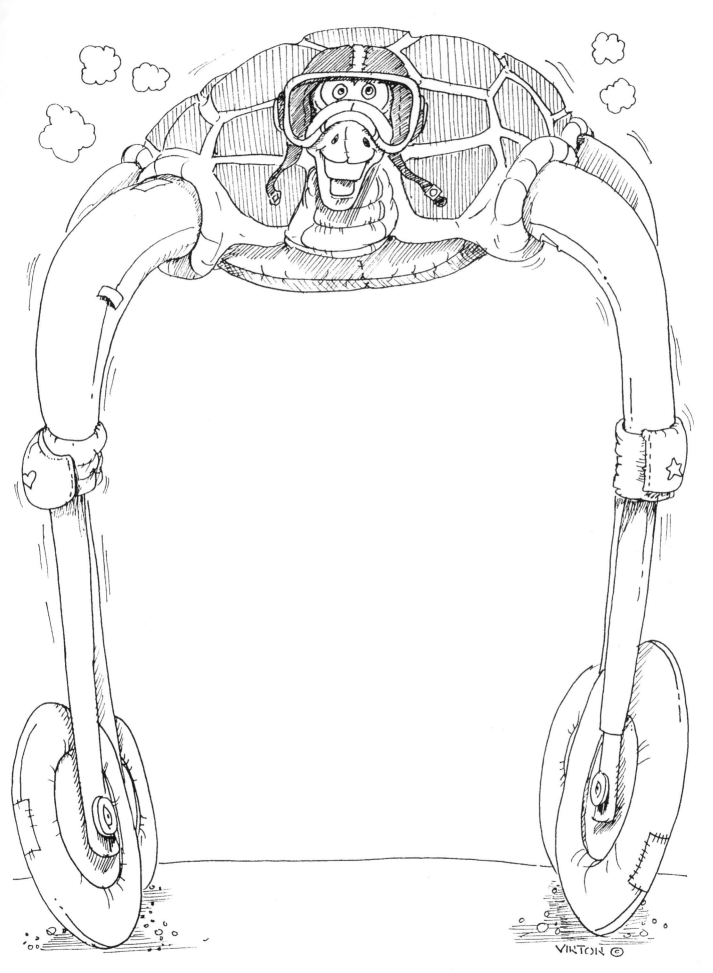

Tick-Tock Critters

"I must govern the clock, not be governed by it."
Golda Meir

Things to Do

What Are They? These critters are actually . . . what? Look carefully at their shapes. What do you see?

Magic Midnight. When the clock strikes 12, these critters come alive for one hour. What do they do? Write a short story.

Your Time. What's your favorite time of the day? Draw more balloon critters (snakes? worms?) to mark the time, then write about why this time is special to you.

One of This, Two of That. For every number on the clock, think of something that comes in that quantity. *Example:* a dozen eggs. Make a list.

The History of Clocks. Research the history of clocks. Use this page to write a brief report about what you learn.

The International Date Line. What is the International Date Line? What interesting event happens there? Find out and write about it.

Who's in Charge? Do you control time . . . or does time control you? Write about at least one way in which you have taken control of your time.

Discussion Questions

- How is military time different from standard time?

- Which do you prefer, an analog clock or a digital clock? Predict the next new type of clock that will be invented.

- Clockwise, counterclockwise—what's the difference?

- What does it mean when "time stands still"? What would happen if time really stood still for five seconds? Five hours? Five days?

81

Cow

*"High diddle diddle
The cat and the fiddle
The cow jumped over the moon."*

Nursery rhyme

Things to Do

Cow Tale. Paul Bunyan had Babe the Blue Ox. Who is this cow? Whose cow is it? What are its special qualities? Create a new folk tale about this cow.

City Cow, Country Cow. This "citified" cow just arrived on the farm. It needs some advice on farm life and etiquette. Write 5–10 helpful tips the cow can follow to fit into its new environment.

Drink Your Milk. Research how milk is purified for drinking by people. Name the different processes that are used and briefly define each one.

Commercial Cow. This cow has been hired by a company that makes athletic shoes. It is going to star in all of the company's commercials. Write the first commercial.

Cow College. Find out and list 10 interesting facts about cows. Put a star by the one that surprised you the most.

Discussion Questions

- Could this cow jump over the moon? Why or why not?

- If you could live anywhere you wanted, would you choose a farm or a city? Explain your answer.

- A poet named Gelett Burgess once wrote, "I never saw a purple cow, I never hope to see one; But I can tell you, anyhow, I'd rather see than be one." Would you rather see one . . . or be one? Why?

Star Dancers

"Dance is the hidden language of the soul."
Martha Graham

Things to Do

Get the Message. These star creatures have come from another planet with an important message for us. Because they don't speak our language, they communicate through dance. What are they saying in this drawing?

Dance Music. Imagine that you can hear the music these creatures are dancing to. Write the melody or the lyrics. Or write about how this music makes you feel.

Dances of the Past. Research dances from the past. Choose one to write about. Start by telling a little about its history. Then give instructions for how to do the dance, using illustrations or words (or both).

Family Dances. Ask a grandparent or another adult about a favorite dance he or she used to do. Use this page to record your interview.

Cave Paintings. Imagine that these drawings were found inside a secret cave. They are millions of years old. What story do they tell?

Discussion Questions

- Do you like to dance? Why or why not?

- Finish this sentence: "Dancing is for _____." Explain your answer. Does it reveal any stereotypes you have about dancers and dancing?

- Have you ever been so happy that you felt like dancing?

- Have you ever been so sad that you felt like dancing?

- Can dance express all kinds of feelings?

Pencils and Pens

"How do I know what I think until I see what I say?"
E.M. Forster

Things to Do

They're Alive! At night, when our school rooms are dark and no one is there, our school tools come alive! Use this page to write about their adventures.

Whose Would You Be? If you were a pen or a pencil, who would you like to belong to? Why? Write about it.

Dreams. If any of these objects (pens, pencils, sharpeners, ink bottle) could dream, what would they dream about? Write a dream or two.

Writing: The Next Generation. It's your job to create the "next generation" writing implement—something beyond a pencil or pen. Draw it and describe it. Write an advertisement for it. Be sure to list the features that make it better than anything else currently on the market.

If They Could Speak . . . . What if pencils or pens could speak? Think of a writing implement that belongs (or belonged) to a famous person. What stories could it tell? Write one of the stories. Use the first person. *Example:* "Einstein picked me up and wrote . . . ."

Research Project. Who invented the pen? The pencil? The eraser? The sharpener? Research one or more of these and write a brief report on your findings.

Discussion Questions

- Does writing help you to think more clearly? Explain.

- What is one thing you do to get in the mood for writing?

- Which do you prefer to write with, a pen or a pencil? Or would you rather do your writing on a computer?

- Do you think that computers will ever totally replace pens or pencils? Why or why not?

Solar System

"Exploration is really the essence of the human spirit."
Astronaut Frank Borman

Things to Do

Mercury, Venus, Earth, or . . . ? Give each planet (including Earth) a new name. Give a reason for each name you choose.

Space Colony. You have been chosen to lead an expedition to colonize another planet. What planet will you colonize? Who will you include in your expedition? What will you bring to your new home? Use this page to write about your plans.

Fascinating Facts. Find out one fascinating fact about each planet in our solar system. Use this page to list your facts.

Space Poetry. Write a poem based on your space research.

A New Solar System. You're a space explorer who has just discovered a new solar system. Write about the heavenly bodies you find.

Planet Personalities. Give each planet on the page a name and a personality. Tell how its personality affects the life on each planet.

Space Spelling. Come up with a list of challenging spelling words about space and space exploration. Include definitions.

Discussion Questions

- What do you know about the sky? The Milky Way? The universe?

- Throughout human history, people have looked to the stars for guidance. Why?

- Do you believe there is life on other planets? Explain your answer.

Stitch It

"A stitch in time saves nine."
Proverb

Things to Do

Proverbs. Explain the meaning of the proverb, "A stitch in time saves nine." Come up with three more proverbs or popular sayings and explain their meanings, too. Or invent a proverb of your own and tell what it means.

Research Project. Research quilts and quilting. Write a brief report on your findings.

Quilt Patterns. Find out about three famous or traditional quilt patterns. Use this page to sketch and describe them.

Quilt Design. Use this page to create your own quilt design. Will it be a patchwork quilt? Will it repeat the same design over and over? Will it be one big scene? What kinds of fabrics will you use? Create your design, color it in, and give it a name.

Stitch It or . . . ? Brainstorm the many different ways we have to fasten things together. *Examples:* stitches, tape, glue, etc. Come up with a new kind of "fastener." Describe it and explain how it works.

Discussion Questions

- Is quilting an art or a craft? Find out the difference, then decide which you think it is. (Teacher: If possible, bring a quilt in to show the class. Discuss the design, the patience, the work, and the time it takes to make a quilt.)

- What are the objects shown at the bottom of the page? What is the function of each one?

- This spool wants to be a javelin thrower. What is a javelin thrower? Can the spool compete in the next Olympic games?

Sounds of Music

"Music is another way of thinking, or maybe thinking is another kind of music."

Ursula K. Le Guin

Things to Do

Music ABC. Create an alphabet book of musical instruments, words, and sounds. Include definitions and illustrations.

Different Drums. What is a timpani? Does it belong in a symphony? Find out and write about the differences between a drum and a timpani, a snare and a bongo.

Concert Tonight! Use this page to write an advertisement for an upcoming concert. It can be any kind of concert you choose.

Jazz. Jazz has been called the only musical form invented in America. Where and when did jazz begin? Research jazz and use this page to write a brief report. Or research one famous jazz musician or singer and report on him or her.

They're Alive! When everyone leaves school for the day, the instruments in the band room come alive. Write about their adventures.

Instant Ability. Imagine that when you wake up tomorrow, you can play any instrument you choose. What will it be and why? Write about it.

Discussion Questions

- Which instrument is your personal favorite? Why do you like it so much?

- What kind of music do you listen to when you're with friends? When you're alone? Is there a difference? Why?

- You're a famous composer, and you've just written a symphony. Who will you dedicate it to? Why?

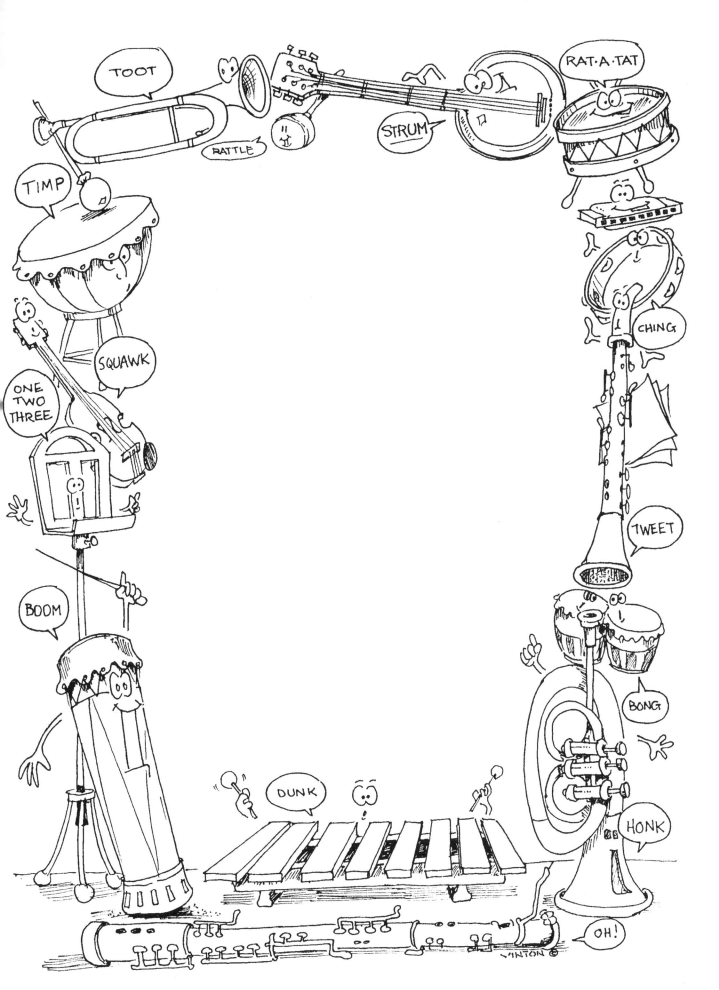

95

Moons and Stars

"Go for the moon. If you don't get it, you'll still be heading for a star."

Willis Reed

Things to Do

Phases of the Moon. What are the phases of the moon? Find out, then write a brief report and illustrate the phases.

Moon Madness. Create a character who becomes a "lunatic" (crazy or foolish) when the moon is full. Write a story about what happens next. Your character can be human, animal, or something else. *Tip:* The word "lunatic" is from the Latin word "luna," meaning "moon."

Moon Facts. Find out and list five fascinating facts or theories about the moon. You might start by asking questions. *Examples:* How can a million-year-old chunk of rock be "new" every month? How do the phases of the moon affect the earth? Where did the moon come from? What is a "blue moon"?

Moon Landing. What were the first words spoken on the moon? Research the first moon landing and use this page to write a brief report. *Trivia Fact:* The first words were really "O.K. . . ." They were followed by the famous words you'll read about in your research.

Discussion Questions

- Would you like to go to the moon someday? If so, what will be the first thing you do when you get there?

- Are you affected by the phases of the moon? Explain your answer.

- Have you ever "reached for the moon"? Did you ever set a very high goal for yourself and achieve it? Tell about this experience.

Beakers and Burners

*"There is an art to science and a science to art;
the two are not enemies, but different aspects of the whole."*

Isaac Asimov

Things to Do

Take a Closer Look. What is a microscope? What is it used for? Who invented it, and why? Find out about this fascinating and useful scientific instrument. List five interesting facts you learn.

Burned Out. A German chemist named Robert Bunsen helped to popularize the gas burner now known as the Bunsen Burner. He also discovered two elements. What were they? Give their names and brief descriptions.

Petri Power. You've succeeded in growing something in the petri dish. What is it called? What is it good for? Use this page to write a lab report describing your experiment.

Slimed! Amoeba, bacteria, plasma, gelatin . . . . What are they? Describe them and tell how they are different.

Pierre and Marie. Pierre and Marie Curie were a famous couple. What did they do? Did they use any of the scientific tools shown in this drawing?

Science Smarts. If you could do any science experiment you wanted, what would it be? Write the steps you would follow to do your experiment.

Science ABC. Create an alphabet book of words, tools, discoveries, and people related to science.

Discussion Questions

- Why do we study science in school? Do you think it's important to study science? Why or why not?

- Is it necessary to dissect frogs to learn about biology? If so, why? If not, what are other ways we can learn about biology?

- Is science safe or dangerous? Explain your answer.

- Do you think the world will ever be free of bacteria and viruses?

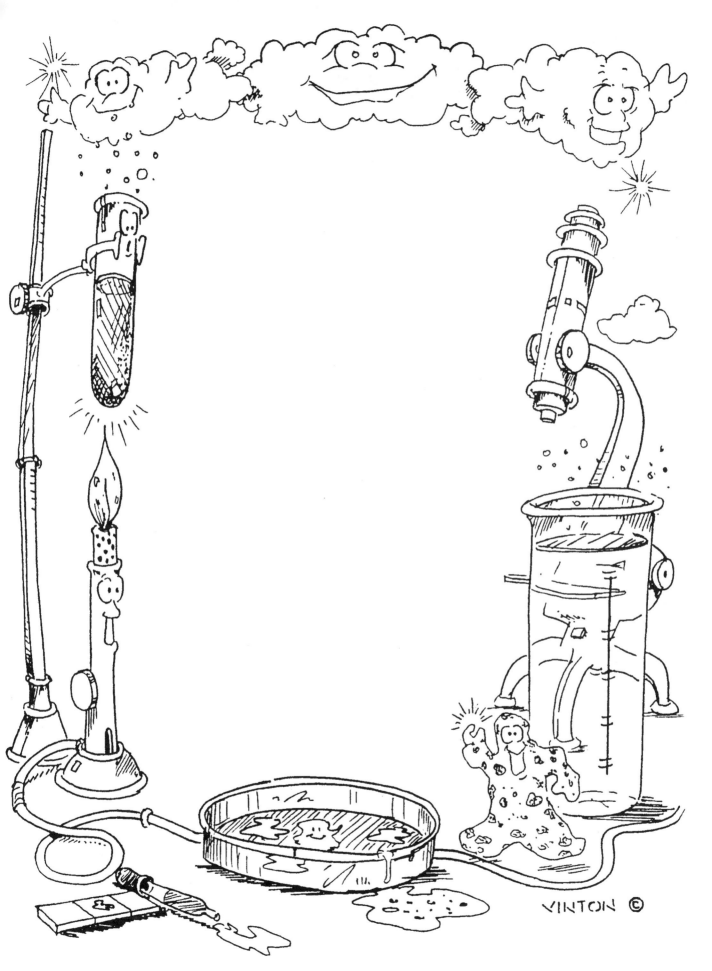

VINTON ©

Carousel

"A horse is a horse, of course, of course."
Theme song for the television program "Mr. Ed"

Things to Do

The Great Escape. This carousel horse has escaped from the amusement park. Where will it go? What will it do? Use this page to write about the horse's adventures.

Magic Merry-Go-Round. You've just climbed onto a carousel horse on a magic merry-go-round. It can go anywhere you want it to. Write about your journey.

Horse Facts. Research two or three different types of horses. List three interesting facts about each one. Or write about one type in more detail.

Carousel Creature. Invent another creature who belongs on a carousel. Draw it and describe it.

Famous Riders. This carousel horse has carried many children over the years. Tell a story about the famous people who rode it when they were young.

Carousel History. Research the history of carousels. Who invented the first one? Where was it? What was the significance of the "brass ring"? About how many carousels are left in the world?

If You Love Horses . . . . Express your feelings in poetry or prose.

Discussion Questions

- What is your favorite carnival or amusement park ride? Why do you enjoy it so much?

- Have you ever ridden a real horse? What was it like?

- Do you think that every town should have a carousel? Why or why not?

- Do carousel horses ever get dizzy?

- When is a horse not a horse?

VINTON ©

Twining Vines

"What is a weed? A plant whose virtues have not yet been discovered."
Ralph Waldo Emerson

Things to Do

A Tale of Three Vines. These three vines were once real people, but they were bewitched by an angry wizard. Use this page to tell their story.

Invent-a-Plant. Invent a new plant or flower. Write about its physical characteristics. Tell what type of environment it needs to grow. Give it a name.

Plant Food. These vines aren't satisfied with ordinary plant food. What do they eat instead? Are they herbivores, carnivores, or omnivores? (If you don't know what those words mean, look them up before you make your decision.)

Up, Up and Away. These vines are distant relatives of the beanstalk Jack grew. Once they break through the top of the page, how high will they grow? Where will they lead to?

Who's the Gardener? Draw the gardener who cares for these remarkable vines.

Discussion Questions

- Do you have a green thumb? Tell about a time when you tried to grow a plant.

- If you could have a garden, what would you grow? (If you do have a garden, what do you grow?)

- If plants could talk, what would they say?

Bones

"A jest breaks no bones."
Samuel Johnson

Things to Do

The Revenge of Mr. Bones. Mr. Bones is very unhappy. Some prankster tied his shoelaces together! Write a short story about "The Revenge of Mr. Bones."

Joints. We have different types of joints on our bodies. Each type has a special function. Find out their names and what they do. Use this page to write a brief report.

Bone Doctors. Look up "orthopedist," "osteopath," and "chiropractor." Write the definitions. How are they different?

Bone Matter. What is bone made of? What are some foods that help to build healthy bones? Use this page to write a menu that's good for the bones.

Rubber Bones. When you woke up this morning, you were surprised to discover that your skeleton had turned to rubber! Use one half of the page to list the good things about this change. Use the other half to list the not-so-good things about it.

Skeleton Smarts. Bone up on the human skeleton. Research it and list at least five interesting facts you find.

Discussion Questions

- Why are skeletons scary?

- What bones are shown in the drawing?

- You've just untied the shoelace holding Mr. Bones's shoes together. What happens next?

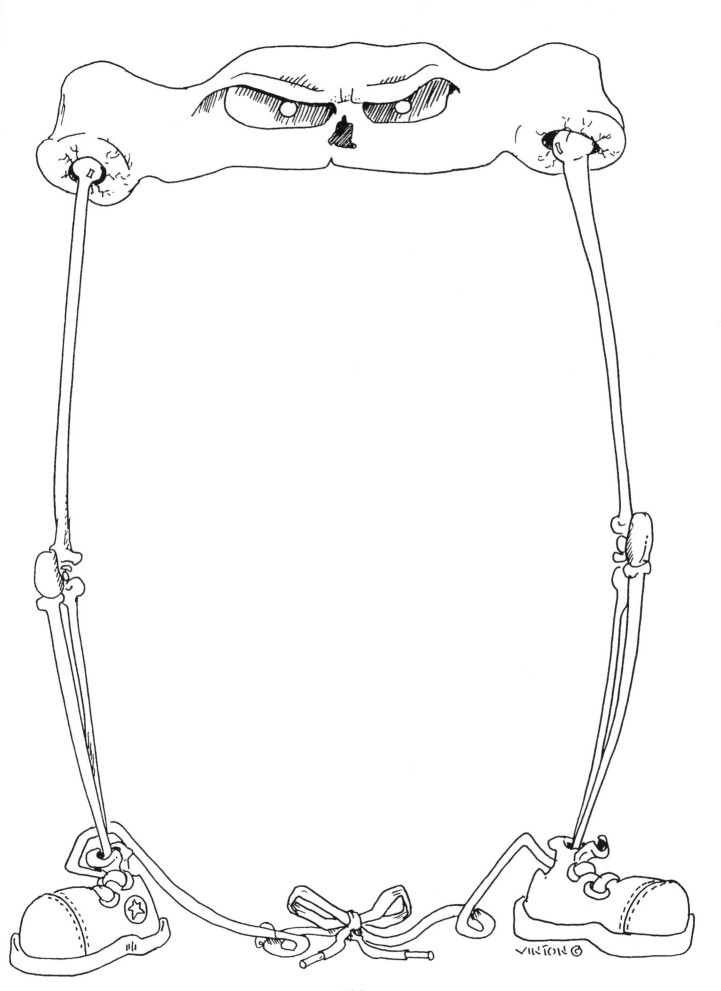

Blocks

"Symbols are the imaginative signposts of life."
Margot Asquith

Things to Do

Could We Live without Them? What would life be like without letters and numbers? How could we write a letter? Read a book? Pay for a purchase? Create a type of communication that doesn't use letters or numbers. Use it to write a short note to a friend.

Start the Presses. Before typesetting equipment and computers, newspapers and books used to be printed with blocks that looked something like the ones shown in the drawing. Research the history of printing and use this page to write a brief report.

The Language of Printing. What is a "printer's devil"? Find out. Then make a list of five more printing words and phrases and write their definition.

Your Name in Type. A "font" is a complete set of type—all letters and numbers—of the same size and design. Create your own font. Write your name in letters from your font.

Who Was He? Who was Johann Gutenberg? Find out and write about his accomplishments.

Discussion Questions

- "Perspective" is the technique of representing three-dimensional objects on a two-dimensional surface, like paper. "Perspective" also means "point of view." What's your perspective on the perspective in this drawing? Why do the blocks look three-dimensional?

- What is a "blockhead"? A "chip off the old block"? A "blockbuster"? A "block party"?

Hydrant and Hoses

"Water is the most precious, limited natural resource we have in this country."
Ralph Nader

Things to Do

Surprise! This is a very special hydrant. When you turn it on, you don't get water. You get . . . what? Cherry cola? Orange juice? Iced tea? Or . . . ? Decide what comes out of the hydrant and how you will use it. Write your story.

Hose Talk. The hose on the right has a problem: It's about to spring a leak! Imagine that you overhear a conversation between the two hoses. Write it down in dialogue.

The Secret World of Water. We seldom think about where water comes from. We just turn on the tap and there it is! Research where the water in your school comes from. Use this page to write a brief report on what you learn.

H$_2$O. Find out how and why hydrogen and oxygen combine to make water. Write about what you learn. Draw a water molecule.

It's Raining, It's Pouring. Where does rain come from? How does it get into the sky? Is it clean when it falls to the ground? What is acid rain? Find answers to these questions and write them on this page.

Water, Water Everywhere. Make a list of all the ways you use water.

Clean Water. You have just been put in charge of cleaning the world's polluted water. What will you do first? Second? Third? Write a press release describing your action plan.

Discussion Questions

- What are you doing to conserve water? What else can you do?

- Why can't people drink sea water?

- Tell about your best time in or on the water. Were you swimming? Canoeing? Zipping down a water slide? Water skiing? Or . . . ?

- Do you want to be a firefighter when you grow up? Why or why not?

Right Writing

"If you wish to be a writer, write."
Epictetus

Things to Do

Be a Writer. Use this page to write anything you please—a poem, a short story, an essay, a letter, or . . . ?

Connections. Write your name in different ways. The only rule is: Every letter must touch at least two other letters.

Homonyms. "Right" and "write" are *homonyms.* They sound the same but have different meanings. Make a list—as long as you can—of other homonyms you can think of or find.

Change Hands. If you're right-handed, try writing or drawing with your left hand. If you're left-handed, use your right hand. Do this every day for a week. Date each writing sample. At the end of the week, check your progress. Has your writing improved? Your drawing? If you like, keep this up for a month or two. With practice, you may become *ambidextrous*—able to use *both* hands for writing and drawing.

Mirror Writing. Write a few sentences in mirror writing. Check your work. Can you find out about any famous people who used mirror writing? *Hint:* Leonardo da Vinci was one.

Letter Writing. Write a letter to a friend or relative you haven't written to for a long time. Mail your letter.

Discussion Questions

- Think of different types of writing—fiction, nonfiction, poetry, plays, novels, short stories, articles, etc. Which do you most like to read? Which do you most like to write?

- Who is your favorite writer? What do you like most about his or her writing?

- Imagine that you've just finished writing a great novel. Say the last sentence out loud.

110

About the Author

Ken Vinton was born on the same date the *Titanic* sank and Abraham Lincoln was shot. Also, he shares his birth date with Pete Rose . . . . Given this "great start," Ken set out to be a little different and walk the path less traveled. He has been a contractor, an antiques dealer, a racquetball pro, and always an artist. He has been an art teacher for 25 years, with a B.S. in Art Education from Indiana University of Pennsylvania and an M.A. in printmaking with a minor in drawing. He enjoys sharing his ideas on creativity in workshops, and he is active in the education and advancement of gifted children. According to him, he lives a "blessed life" with his family—wife Mary Ann (a third grade teacher), children Ali and Ryan, and two Cocker Spaniels, Inxs and Majic—in an idyllic town in Pennsylvania.

Ken is a popular and experienced workshop presenter and motivational speaker. Workshop topics include:

- Creativity
- Cartooning
- Writing with Pictures
- Illustration

If you're interested in contacting Ken about working with teachers in your district, please call or write:

Ken Vinton c/o Free Spirit Publishing Inc.
400 First Avenue North, Suite 616
Minneapolis, MN 55401-1724
Telephone (612) 338-2068

Other Great Books from Free Spirit

Alphabet Antics
Hundreds of Activities to Challenge and Enrich Letter Learners of All Ages
written and illustrated by Ken Vinton, M.A.
This fresh, inventive approach to the ABC's promotes creativity, stimulates curiosity, and invites exploration and discovery through activities and illustrated, reproducible handouts. For grades K–6.
$19.95; 144 pp.; softcover; illus.; 8½" x 11"

Challenging Projects for Creative Minds
12 Self-Directed Enrichment Projects That Develop and Showcase Student Ability
for Grades 1–5
by Phil Schlemmer, M.Ed., and Dori Schlemmer
The best way to prepare children for the future is to teach them how to learn, and that's just what these projects do. Each project sparks kids' imaginations, calls on their creativity, and challenges them to solve problems, find and use information, and think for themselves. For teachers, grades 1–5.
$29.95; 144 pp.; softcover; illus.; 8½" x 11"

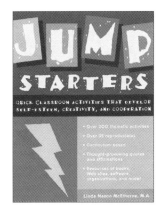

Jump Starters
Quick Classroom Activities That Develop Self-Esteem, Creativity, and Cooperation
by Linda Nason McElherne, M.A.
Make the most of every minute in your classroom by keeping this book close at hand. Features fifty-two themes within five topics: Knowing Myself, Getting to Know Others, Succeeding in School, Life Skills, and Just for Fun. For teachers, grades 3–6.
$21.95; 184 pp.; softcover; illus.; 8½" x 11"

Building Self-Esteem Through the Museum of I
25 Original Projects That Explore and Celebrate the Self
by Linda R. Zack, M.Ed.
The student-centered, open-ended activities in this book encourage divergent, original thinking and allow creative expression in varied media and forms. Includes dozens of reproducible handout masters. For grades 4–8.
$18.95; 144 pp.; softcover; illus.; 8½" x 11"

To place an order or to request a free catalog of SELF–HELP FOR KIDS® and SELF–HELP FOR TEENS® materials, please write, call, email, or visit our Web site:

Free Spirit Publishing Inc.
400 First Avenue North • Suite 616 • Minneapolis, MN 55401-1724
toll-free 800.735.7323 • local 612.338.2068 • fax 612.337.5050
help4kids@freespirit.com • www.freespirit.com